Y0-EGH-191

THE SCOOP ON ICE CREAM

JULIE KNUTSON

CHERRY LAKE PRESS

Published in the United States of America by Cherry Lake Publishing Group
Ann Arbor, Michigan
www.cherrylakepublishing.com

Reading Adviser: Reading Adviser: Beth Walker Gambro, MS, Ed., Reading Consultant, Yorkville, IL
Photo Credits: © nuiiko/iStock.com, cover, 1; © drewstock/Shutterstock.com, 5; © Everret Collection/
    Shutterstock.com, 6; © MidoSemsem/Shutterstock.com, 8; © MM Stock/Shutterstock.com, 9;
    © Brent Hofacker/Shutterstock.com, 10, 14; © Bartosz Luczak/Shutterstock.com, 13; © MTaitas/
    Shutterstock.com, 17; © FatCamera/iStock.com, 18; © Vladimir Razgulyaev/Shutterstock.com, 21;
    © Kat Peterson/iStock.com, 23; © hdagli/iStock.com, 24; © Konstantin Kolosov/Shutterstock.com, 27;
    © sandoclr/iStock.com, 28

Cherry Lake Press is an imprint of Cherry Lake Publishing Group.

Library of Congress Cataloging-in-Publication Data

Names: Knutson, Julie, author.
Title: The scoop on ice cream / by Julie Knutson.
Description: Ann Arbor, Michigan : Cherry Lake Publishing, [2022] | Series: The dish on the dish: a history
    of your favorite foods | Includes index. | Audience: Grades 4-6
Identifiers: LCCN 2021006132 (print) | LCCN 2021006133 (ebook) | ISBN 9781534187351 (hardcover) |
    ISBN 9781534188754 (paperback) | ISBN 9781534190153 (pdf) | ISBN 9781534191556 (ebook)
Subjects: LCSH: Ice cream, ices, etc.–History–Juvenile literature.
Classification: LCC TX795 .K524 2021 (print) | LCC TX795 (ebook) | DDC 641.86/2–dc23
LC record available at https://lccn.loc.gov/2021006132
LC ebook record available at https://lccn.loc.gov/2021006133

Cherry Lake Publishing Group would like to acknowledge the work of the Partnership for 21st Century
Learning, a Network of Battelle for Kids. Please visit http://www.battelleforkids.org/networks/p21
for more information.

Printed in the United States of America
Corporate Graphics

ABOUT THE AUTHOR

Julie Knutson is an author who lives in northern Illinois with her husband, son, and border
collie. She prefers her pancakes with Nutella and bananas, her pizza "Detroit-style," and her
mac 'n' cheese with little green peas.

TABLE OF CONTENTS

CHAPTER 1

First Plating

It comes in endless varieties, from vintage vanilla to wacky white chocolate habanero. You can dress it up with whipped cream and a cherry on top for a special sundae. Or you can pair it with root beer for a frothy float. It's brought delight to people of all ages. In all corners of the globe, it's the ultimate summertime sweet.

You guessed it! It's the near-universal treat for which we all scream . . . ICE CREAM!

So, what's the scoop on ice cream? When and where was it invented? Who were the geniuses who dreamed up this happy marriage of frozen dairy and sugar? And how did it spread around the world?

The most popular ice cream flavor in the United States is chocolate.

Ice cream releases serotonin in the brain, which makes you feel happy!

Like so many of the foods we enjoy, ice cream's path to our bowls took many routes on multiple continents. Whether in ancient China, the Persian Empire, or **Renaissance** Italy, people craved ways to cool off with chilled treats. So determining its actual origin is tough, if not impossible. But there are a few points on which food historians and **anthropologists** tend to agree. Let's take a look at what archaeological and written records reveal about how ice cream came to be. As far back as 3000 BCE, wealthy people in China, India, and the Middle East sent their servants to the mountains to harvest ice and snow. These hauls were stored in underground, straw-lined chambers to keep them in a solid state. Archaeologists have uncovered evidence of ice pits in ancient Babylon that date to the 2nd century BCE. Writings show that rulers ranging from King Solomon to Alexander the Great enjoyed

A Dangerous Substance... Or A Cure for What Ails You?

The ancient Greek physician Hippocrates took a strong stand against cold foods. He said that ice, snow, and other cold substances caused coughing and inflammation of the chest. His ideas were followed for centuries. Early medical writers and dietitians claimed that cold foods and drinks interfered with the function of the body's **humors**. People thought they could cause a number of illnesses, from blindness to sudden death. The view changed as ice cream became more popular. By 1775, Italian physician Fillipo Baldini supported eating ices and ice cream. As historian Jeri Quinzio explains, Baldini felt that "The combination of sugar, salt, and cold was infinitely beneficial to our bodies." His final conclusion? From gout to depression, ice cream was the cure.

Alexander the Great also enjoyed snow and ice flavored with honey and nectar.

drinks chilled with ice. How did these ancient leaders prefer their chilled beverages? Alexander took his with honey or wine!

The first evidence of mixing ice with dairy stems to China's Tang Dynasty, which reigned from 618 to 907 CE. According to food historians, milk from a buffalo, cow, or goat was combined with flour and **camphor** to create a thickened texture and unique flavor. Then, the mixture was placed in metal tubes that were submerged in ice water until the substance froze.

The ideal temperature for storing ice cream is
0 degrees Fahrenheit (–18 degrees Celsius).

Rainbow sherbet was invented by Emanuel Goren in the 1950s.

During medieval times on the Arabian Peninsula, frozen drinks flavored with fruits such as pomegranate, quince, and cherry gained favor. Traders brought these **sherbet**-like treats to the Mediterranean. From there, they spread throughout Europe. Ice was precious and expensive, so the cold treats were largely limited to the wealthy.

Naples, Italy, was *the place* where ice cream as we know it came of age. In 1558, scholar Giambattista della Porta wrote a book explaining that ice laced with salt could be used to freeze wine and milk, which have freezing points below that of water. About 100 years later, chef Antonio Latini ushered in the shift from frozen drinks to frozen desserts that used sugar for added sweetness. Latini is credited with creating the first milk **sorbet**.

Early forms of ice cream quickly spread across Europe. In 1686, Paris' Café Procope opened its doors. Fashionable Parisians and visitors to the city crowded into the café to sip coffee and spoon ice cream. Café Procope is still open today, claiming the title of Paris' oldest operating cafe.

CHAPTER 2

Migrations

There's a myth that Martha Washington accidentally invented ice cream. As the story goes, Washington left a bowl of sweet cream out overnight. The cream froze. The next morning, she was greeted with a delectable twist-of-fate. In this story, ice cream was born on the grounds of Mount Vernon, making it a uniquely American invention.

Of course, we know that ice cream was enjoyed well before the Washingtons, in earlier centuries and on other continents. But a story connecting the first president's family and ice cream isn't surprising, as George Washington *absolutely loved* the stuff. President Thomas Jefferson also couldn't get enough of it. He is the author of one of the first written recipes for ice cream in the

Thomas Jefferson used vanilla beans in his ice cream recipe.

United States. At his estate, Jefferson had multiple ice houses to store ices and creams. First Lady Dolley Madison ordered that ice cream be served at the inauguration of her husband, President James Madison. Her favorite flavor? Oyster!

Because of the steep price of ice, sugar, and salt, ice cream remained an elite treat for many years. But by the early 1800s, residents of New York and Boston, Massachusetts, could go to "pleasure gardens" to stroll well-kept lawns, admire flowering plants, sip lemonade, and eat ice cream. While flavors like vanilla,

The first root beer float was invented in 1893.

chocolate, and strawberry were popular, more unusual offerings like soft-boiled egg sweetened with brown sugar were also on the menu. Elsewhere, ice cream saloons and creameries sprung up to meet the growing appetite for the sweet stuff. In Philadelphia, Pennsylvania, during the 1830s and 1840s, former White House chef Augustus Jackson became a well-known caterer, **confectioner**, and ice cream-maker. He was one of the city's wealthiest African American residents. Ice cream peddlers used pushcarts to sell cold treats on city and town streets. Eager children followed them.

What led ice cream to reach more people in this time period? Technological changes that came with the **Industrial Revolution** were the key. These changes included better refrigeration and freezing techniques, as well as quicker transportation and more efficient production. In 1843, Philadelphian Nancy Johnson got a **patent** for a hand-cranked ice cream maker. Johnson's "artificial freezer" allowed ice cream to be made at a faster rate and with a smoother texture. The basic design of Johnson's device remains largely unchanged today. Additional shifts in ice production and sugar refining also drove prices down. In 1851, the world's first commercial ice cream factory opened in Baltimore, Maryland.

While ice cream became more popular in the 19th and 20th centuries, not all Americans had equal access to it. In her autobiography, I Know Why the Caged Bird Sings, *Maya Angelou wrote, "People in Stamps used to say that the whites in our town were so prejudiced that a Negro couldn't buy vanilla ice cream. Except on July Fourth." This statement was meant to show the hardships of being Black in a* **segregated** *South. While Black people still could purchase ice cream, they had to order from a separate window or door and could be refused service just because of their skin color.*

By the 1860s, ice cream was becoming cheaper and more widely available worldwide.

In the early 20th century, ice cream consumption in the United States skyrocketed. Its popularity was also connected to the **temperance** movement and **Prohibition**. With alcohol being forbidden, ice cream became more widely accepted. Soda fountains serving an array of sundaes, sodas, banana splits, milkshakes, malts, and floats became mainstays of many towns.

Where and when was the first ice cream sundae invented? That question has sparked a fierce rivalry between three towns: Ithaca, New York; Evanston, Illinois; and Two Rivers, Wisconsin. Town leaders and citizens have argued the issue for years. They have written sundae-themed "fight songs," started letter campaigns, and performed research to settle the matter. But no answers have yet been reached.

[21ST CENTURY SKILLS LIBRARY]

Cones come in different varieties, including sugar, cake, and waffle.

When scoop met cone at the 1904 Saint Louis World's Fair in Missouri, ice cream soared to new levels of popularity. As the story goes, it was a sweltering summer day. After one of the fair's ice cream vendors ran out of dishes, his waffle-making neighbor Ernest Hamwi came to the rescue with a waffle cone for serving.

But visual and written evidence suggests that the fair wasn't the first time ice cream was served in a cone. An 1807 drawing shows a woman in a Paris, France, café eating ice cream from a coronet-like cone. A British cookbook from 1846 called for ices to be served

Ice cream trucks are still in operation today.

in cones. In 1901, a patent was issued in England for an "apparatus for baking biscuit-cups for ice-cream." A similar application was filed in New York in 1902. As with ice cream itself, it seems that its companion cone sprung in many places within a matter of decades.

In the following years, changes in how and where people enjoyed ice cream reflected shifts in the culture at large. During the hard times of the **Great Depression**, people sought out cheap 5-cent ice cream treats. As cars became more popular in the 1930s and 1940s, roadside stands serving soft-serve ice cream gained popularity. After World War II, the United States enjoyed a period of prosperity. Many families moved into houses in the **suburbs**, where empty freezers and refrigerators waited to be filled. Ice cream manufacturers responded with gallon-sized containers that lined supermarket freezers. Home cooks were encouraged to transform these into dazzling desserts like the Baked Alaska, an impressive combination of ice cream and cake topped with **meringue**.

Ice Cream Trucks on the Move!

Let's face it—ice cream can be messy. In the early 1920s, Ohioan Harry Burt set off to solve this problem with the invention of the Good Humor® Ice Cream Sucker. It was later known as the Good Humor® bar. At the suggestion of his son, Burt put the bar of chocolate-coated ice cream on a wooden stick. This made eating ice cream less of a sticky mess.

But he didn't stop there. By the end of the 1920s, Burt operated a fleet of refrigerated trucks. These modern ice cream mobiles allowed vendors to meet customers where they were on hot summer days. The trucks not only rang bells to alert hungry kids, but they also played catchy tunes.

CHAPTER 3

Evolution and Wild Variations

Around the world, ice cream continues to evolve. Chefs blend ancient traditions and classic recipes with novel flavors and presentations. Let's take a round-the-world trip to see what you can enjoy in different places!

Our journey starts in Idaho. Snag yourself an ice cream potato at Boise's West Side Drive In. Don't worry—it's not really a starchy vegetable stuffed with ice cream. Instead, it's vanilla ice cream shaped into a potato form and dusted with cocoa powder.

Thai rolled ice cream starts off as a liquid and
then is rolled on a freezing surface.

Hop on a plane and jet across the Pacific Ocean! In Japan, check out **mochi**, an ice cream treat made with sticky rice. Still hungry? Head south to Singapore and score yourself an ice cream sandwich. What makes this one unique? It's literally a slice of soft sandwich bread folded around a brick of ice cream.

Next up is India, where you can sample **kulfi**. This sweet treat is most often made from condensed milk and sweetened with flavors like rosewater and mango. Head northwest to Iran to try **faloodeh**, a crunchy noodle sorbet. Carry on to Turkey, where you can enjoy a slice of taffy-like **dondurma** cut fresh from a slab by a market vendor.

Feeling adventurous? Head to the Freakybuttrue Pecularium in Portland, Oregon. The Pecularium serves up a "Bug Eater's Delight" sundae topped with crickets, scorpions, mealworms, whipped cream, and chocolate sauce.

Mochi is extremely popular around New Year,
because it is a symbol of good fortune.

Gelato comes in many flavors, including hazelnut, coffee, and pistachio.

Keep heading north to Germany. A bowl of "Spaghettieis"—ice cream masquerading as a giant plate of spaghetti with tomato sauce—is sure to cause a bit of confusion about whether you're enjoying dinner or dessert. No ice cream tour would be complete without a stop in Naples, Italy, widely regarded as the birthplace of **gelato**.

Continue your travels south to Cape Town, South Africa. The city's Unframed Ice Cream shop is regarded as one of the best in the world. It makes ice cream from real and **sustainable** ingredients. Take your cone of chocolate tahini or double carrot cake and check out the Boulders Beach penguins!

To close the trip, zip across the Atlantic to Ecuador. Lend a hand in making **helado de paila**, ice cream hand-crafted in a giant bronze bowl. If you're done with dairy at this point, you can enjoy it as a tropical, milk-free sorbet.

CHAPTER 4

Make Your Own!

Try your hand at making ice cream in a bag!

INGREDIENTS:

- 1 cup (237 milliliters) half-and-half
- 2 tablespoons (25 grams) granulated sugar
- ½ teaspoon (2.8 g) pure vanilla extract
- 3 cups (384 g) ice
- ⅓ cup (43 g) kosher salt

Today, they make special ice creams that are safe for dogs.

DIRECTIONS:

1. Combine the half-and-half, sugar, and vanilla in a small resealable bag. Push out the air and seal tightly!

2. Place the ice and salt in a larger resealable bag.

3. Put the smaller bag inside the larger one. Shake for 7 to 10 minutes, or until the liquid turns to a solid.

4. Scoop out the ice cream and enjoy!

Milkshakes became popular in 1922 and continue to be a delicious treat.

10 Brain-Freezing Facts About Ice Cream

- In the scorching summer of 1790, President George Washington spent a whopping $200 on ice cream. That's about $5,000 in today's money.

- In the 1960s, Cuban leader Fidel Castro built a massive ice cream parlor to seat 1,000 people. Named Coppelia, the parlor still dishes out treats for customers today.

- What country consumes the most ice cream? A January 2020 report showed that New Zealand takes the title. Each resident scoops up about 7.5 gallons (28.4 liters) per year.

- In 2015, a Norwegian team constructed the world's tallest ice cream cone. The towering structure measured 10 feet (3 meters) tall!

- Mochi ice cream was actually invented in the United States by Japanese-American businesswoman Frances Hashimoto.

- The Florida State Fair's "Fried Ice Cream Burger" tops a mound of beef, bacon, cheese, lettuce, onion, pickle, and tomato with—you guessed it!—a scoop of fried vanilla.

- While freeze-dried "astronaut ice cream" was created for the first *Apollo* mission in 1969, the edible invention didn't actually make it into orbit.

- Gelato has less milk fat than ice cream and is typically served 10 to 15 degrees Fahrenheit (–12.2 to –9.4° C) warmer than its colder cousin.

- The first account of ice cream being served in the United States dates to 1744. A guest of the governor of Maryland wrote about being served the frozen treat.

- Competitive eater Miki Sudo holds the world record for ice cream-eating. In 2017, Sudo ate a whopping 16.5 pints (7.8 L) of ice cream in 6 minutes. Brain freeze, anyone?

Timeline

300 BCE   Ice is harvested from mountaintops to cool drinks. Leaders including Alexander the Great enjoy chilled beverages, storing ice in underground chambers insulated with straw.

907 CE   During the Tang Dynasty in China, mixtures of milk, flour, and camphor are encased in metal tubes and submerged in ice. This technique makes for a solid, frozen treat.

1400s   Thanks to traders, during the medieval period, sherbets become popular in the Arabian Peninsula and spread to Europe.

1600s   In Naples, Italy, chef Antonio Latini creates a recipe for a "milk sorbet," paving the way toward ice cream as we know it.

1686   Café Procope opens in Paris, bringing ice cream to France's wealthiest citizens.

1843   Nancy Johnson invents the ice cream churn. Variations of the device are still used today.

1851   The first commercial ice cream factory opens in Baltimore, Maryland.

1920s   In Youngstown, Ohio, Good Humor® trucks make ice cream officially mobile.

1945   During World War II, the U.S. military commissions a barge that serves as a floating ice cream factory and parlor. It serves thousands of soldiers on the Pacific Front.

1988   Dippin' Dots™—ice cream flash frozen into tiny balls by liquid nitrogen—are invented.

Further Reading

BOOKS

Bernard, Jan. *Ice Cream before the Store.* Mankato, MN: The Child's World, 2012.

Knutson, Julie. *From Cow to Cone.* Ann Arbor, MI: Cherry Lake Publishing, 2019.

Rosenberg, Pam. *How Did that Get to My Table? Ice Cream.* Ann Arbor, MI: Cherry Lake Publishing, 2010.

WEBSITES

PBS—Explore The Delicious History of Ice Cream
www.pbs.org/food/the-history-kitchen/explore-the-delicious-history-of-ice-cream
Learn more about the history of ice cream.

Wonderopolis—What Is Gelato?
www.wonderopolis.org/wonder/What-Is-Gelato
Check out this website to learn about gelato.

GLOSSARY

anthropologists (an-thruh-PAH-luh-jists) people who study the norms and values of societies

camphor (KAM-fuhr) oil extracted from an evergreen tree

confectioner (kuhn-FEK-shuh-nuhr) a person who makes candy or other sweets

dondurma (DON-duhr-muh) a taffy-like Turkish ice cream

faloodeh (fuh-LUH-day) Persian sorbet that includes crunchy vermicelli noodles

gelato (jeh-LAH-toh) a dense ice cream common in Italy, with a lower fat content

Great Depression (GRAYT di-PRESH-uhn) the period of global economic decline that lasted from 1929 until 1939

helado de paila (eh-LAH-doh DAY PAY-lah) hand-crafted Ecuadorian ice cream made in a bronze pot

humors (HYOO-muhrs) the fluid substances of the body

Industrial Revolution (in-DUHSS-tree-uhl rev-uh-LOO-shuhn) the large social and economic shift toward machine and factory-produced goods

kulfi (KUHL-fee) a frozen dairy dessert from the Indian subcontinent

meringue (muh-RANG) a stiff mixture of beaten egg whites and sugar

mochi (MOH-chee) an ice cream roll filled with sticky rice

patent (PAH-tuhnt) the legal right to ownership of an invention

Prohibition (proh-uh-BIH-shuhn) the period in which alcohol was banned in the United States

Renaissance (REH-nuh-sahnss) the period of "rebirth" in European history spanning from the 14th through the 17th centuries

segregated (seg-ruh-GAY-tuhd) kept apart because of race

sherbet (SHUHR-buht) a frozen dessert with fruit juice and milk or cream and sugar

sorbet (sor-BAY) a frozen dessert flavored with fruit juice or water and sugar

suburbs (SUHB-urbs) small communities near large cities

sustainable (suh-STAY-nuh-buhl) able to be reproduced at a certain rate, good for the environment

temperance (TEM-puh-ruhnss) the movement to ban alcohol

INDEX